Sexuality and Aging

OLDER ADULT ISSUES SERIES

The Office of Older Adult Ministry of the Presbyterian Church (U.S.A.) and Geneva Press are grateful for the generous gifts of many individuals, congregations, and organizations that helped make possible the publication of this series.

Sexuality and Aging

Rhona M. Jones

Published for the Office of Older Adult Ministry,
A Ministry of the General Assembly Council,
Presbyterian Church (U.S.A.)

Geneva Press
Louisville, Kentucky

Contents

Introduction

The intention of this book is to briefly explore the nature of human sexuality in the later years of life. There are books that consider in detail the physiological changes that occur in older adults and how these changes can impact some aspects of sexual activity. While reference will be made to genital sexual activity, this book will focus more on exploring sexuality as an integral part of the human being. Aging is part of the life pilgrimage all humans make, and sexuality, an integral part of our being from birth, goes with us to death.

I am convinced that in speaking about human beings as sexual beings we must consider spirituality. Sexuality and spirituality seem to me to be two sides of one coin. Because we are embodied beings (male and female), all our thinking, speaking, and experiencing is permeated by our sexuality. Therefore, when I think of, speak of, and experience other human beings, or God, I do so from within my personhood, which includes my sexuality.

My working definition of human sexuality is necessarily broad. As a gift of God's creation I would argue that we neglect consideration of our sexuality at the peril of our wholeness as humans. Just as we know ourselves only in relation to other human beings and God (this is how personhood is conferred), so it is with our sexuality.

James Nelson has described sexuality in this way:

> Sexuality is a sign, a symbol, and a means of our call to communication and communion. This is the most apparent in regard to other human beings, other body-selves. The mystery of our sexuality is the mystery of our need to reach out to embrace others both physically and spiritually. Sexuality thus expresses God's intention that we find our authentic humanness in relationship.[1]

Sexuality is often confused with genital sex, yet this is but *one* expression of our sexuality. There are myriad other ways to express our sexuality. Because sexuality is so personal, and often quite difficult to talk about, many older adults find themselves locked into the place of being less than who they were intended to be as created human beings. Myths, misconceptions, attitudes of young and old, circumstances, and societal pressures all combine to perpetuate this captivity. The church, the community of men and women who are the body of Christ (Christ embodied in the past, present, and future), is in a unique position to redress this situation.

Personal Reflection and Group Discussion
At the end of each section, questions for personal reflection and group discussion are suggested.

1. If you have chosen to read this book as a personal study, it might be helpful to write your responses to the questions/cases studies. Regard this as a journal, a well-tried spiritual exercise. As a record of present reflective thoughts and feelings it can be usefully returned to at a later date.

2. If you have chosen to read this book with others, take some time to think through and write your responses before engaging in discussion. Our sexuality is so much part of our being and so very personal. Often times it is much easier to let the experiences and opinions of others be our reticent voice. Venture to record your *own* feelings and thoughts. They are a starting point and your expression of humanness.

Summary

Chapter 1 explores further the nature of the human being as sexual being. Much of what is said could apply to a person throughout life's seasons. Some expressions of our sexuality grow less intense as we age. This is merely a shift of focus, not a lessening of need to express ourselves as sexual beings. Chapter 2 explores aspects of our sexuality as they relate to sexual behavior and senses. Chapter 3 addresses the relational implications of our study for couples, singles, retirement communities, adult children, and churches. Notes are followed by suggestions for further reading.

1 Human Beings—Sexual and Spiritual

This story is well-worn, but bears another telling. A third grader came home from school with a burning question, "Mom, what is sex?" Mom knew the question would come one day, but she didn't think it would come this soon. Thinking fast about where to begin she started, "Your mom and your dad love one another very much and when two people love one another very much . . ." The third grader listened with due attention. Mom reached a stopping place and inquired, "So, now do you understand about sex?" The small child paused, thought with a wrinkled brow and then said. "Ye-es. I think so. But the box is so small and I have only two letters from which to choose—M or F. Which one does all that come under?"

The confusing ways in which we use the word *sex* and our societal preoccupation with matters of sexual activity can mean many of us are wary of considering carefully and prayerfully, alone or in the presence of others, that aspect of our humanness which is fundamental to our created-ness—sexuality. The ways in which we know ourselves to be male and female, and the ways we express our maleness or femaleness, are an integral part of our sexuality. We are creatures of the flesh and therefore we encounter the world through our bodies. This seems so obvious it is almost ludicrous to spell it out. However, the implications are profound. We cannot *be* in the world other than in our bodies. All our being, our very aliveness, has an underlying dimension of sexuality. Our sexuality cannot be divorced from our creatureliness and our sexuality is not confined to particular genital acts.

A person who chooses to live a celibate life is not a non-sexual being. Neither are persons who find themselves widowed or divorced. Sexuality is fundamental to our humanness. The human need to be in relationship, what Nelson describes as "communication and communion," will, whatever our chronological age, necessarily involve our embodiment. The ways in which we understand and express ourselves as *male* and *female*, including the characteristics which society has defined as *masculine* and *feminine*, are shared by both genders and are not the sole preserve of either men or women.

Christian faith has at its heart the marvelous affirmation of embodiment—"the Word became flesh." All that is God-ness inhabits all that is human, including sexual being. God's reconciling love in Jesus occurred within embodiment and still occurs within embodiment. We receive that love in our body-selves and love's presence ever seeks to make us whole, more fully human, and more fully embodied. Salvation is intimately connected to embodiment. Yet the history of the church is littered with attempts to avoid this reality with a dualism that divides body and soul; declaring the soul is nearer to God than the body. In addition, Christian theologies and liturgies, while using the language of embodiment, have been hampered by ancient and deeply embedded sexual stereotypes.

Christian suspicion of the sexual, perhaps on the one hand a reaction to the deification and incorporation of sexual acts in worship, and on the other hand a recognition of the pervasiveness and powerfulness of sexuality, has meant the church has tended to link sex with sin. Sexuality became an aspect of the human being that needed to be policed and controlled. The questions asked of the scriptures were about what was and was not allowed. Although the Reformers did elevate the role of marriage and sex within marriage, it is only fairly recently that theology has begun to ask fundamental questions about the nature of the human being (sexual and spiritual) as created in the image of God, and how this is illuminated by scripture.

Theology is asking these questions during a time of flux. The medical advances that gave society the pill, and other forms of contraception, heralded the so-called sexual revolution of the 1960s. We are in the midst of changing patterns of relating. New configurations of family and relationships are appearing. The church must formulate a careful response to these changing patterns, since it seems individualism may have paved the way for a transience in relationship that can debase the grace-fullness of our God-given sexuality.

The past decades have also seen Western society place worth and value on productivity. The partner of productivity has shown itself to be consumerism. The subtleties of marketing speak volumes, particularly to older adults. Bombarded by a media advocating a youthful body and beautiful culture, we can be forgiven for thinking that sexuality belongs to the young. In my country, the United Kingdom (England), there has been intense media interest in both the drug Viagra and the IVF treatment that a woman in her sixties traveled to Italy to receive. While both interventions raise questions in the area of medical ethics, I find myself wondering about the link between sexuality and the aging process. In both cases there are questions about performance. In a youth-driven culture, our changing bodies are a reminder of our mortality.

The natural processes of aging do not mean men and women become non-sexual beings. Our sexuality, an integral part of our humanness and a gift at birth, remains with us all our lives. Communication and communion, that "being in relationship" which is the nature of God in whose image we are created, is going to necessarily involve our sexuality at every age or stage, for it is at once both spiritual and physical. While sexuality must not be over-estimated (sexuality does permeate our being alive but is not the whole of our being alive), neither must we under-estimate sexuality. All societies in various periods in human history have grappled with the questions sexuality raises and how those questions find religious expression. Paul Ricoeur identifies three major stages in the Western understanding of the relation of religion to sexuality: (1) the incorporating of sexuality into religious myth and ritual; (2) the separation of sexuality and the sacred which confined sexuality to the "earthly order"; and (3) the more recent trend that seeks to reunite sexuality with the experience of the sacred.[2]

Ricoeur's broad generalization is useful, although Protestant churches from about the nineteenth century onward did develop a hymnody which could best be described as devotional in nature. Favorite gospel hymns, choruses, and quite a few modern hymns have followed this trend. We may have smiled to see Whoopi Goldberg conducting *My God* to a foot-tapping congregation in the movie *Sister Act*, but the Christian church is no stranger to singing love songs to God. It is perhaps simply that now is the time to articulate more intentionally this aspect of our being and faith.

Questions for Thought and Discussion

1. What were the messages or stories you were told as a child about the word "sex"?
2. How do you understand these messages or stories now?
3. What bearing, if any, have these messages or stories had on your own understanding of yourself as a sexual person and your own adult sex life?
4. Have you really thought about the fact that you are in a body and therefore are a sexual being?
5. What does this say to you about the Incarnation, and about your faith in Jesus the Christ?
6. How much of your sex life is governed by what you have been told by society, by what you see on

television or read in magazines, and by the references to sex in later life found in many birthday cards?

7. When is sex sinful, and when is it seen as "the nature of a human person made in the image of God"?

8. How can the new configurations of family be responded to by the church without debasing the grace-fullness of God-given sexual personhood?

9. If performance is the youthful view of sexual activity, what can the vision of sexual activity for the older person be?

10. Which of Paul Ricoeur's stages in understanding the relationship between religion and sexuality fits your beliefs?

11. Are there contemporary hymns or choruses that you can think of that strike you as love songs? What difference is there between these and modern secular love songs?

12. How have the changes in family and personal circumstances in your own life altered how you relate to others?

13. How do you feel about how your body has changed in appearance in the aging process?

14. What new questions about sexuality might baby boomers ask, since they have experienced sexual liberation in our society?

2   Aspects of Sexuality Explored

In this chapter we shall consider some practical in-the-body experiences that relate to both our aging and our sexuality. We begin with the confident affirmation that sexuality and the human need to express love in relationship does not diminish with age. The natural processes of aging may mean the intensity and urgency of expressing our sexuality and love in genital sexual activity changes; however, the need to communicate and commune never wanes.

It is not the intention of this book to detail the physiological changes that occur in our bodies as we age. Changes do occur, but these need not affect sexual functioning. Medical practitioners are increasingly available to give guidance. Taking the step of seeking help may reveal that what we considered to be an enormous and deeply embarrassing problem has a simple explanation and remedy. Above all, contrary to the many myths that are regularly peddled, adults who have enjoyed an active sex life are more than likely to continue to do so in late and very late life. Understanding what happens to our bodies as we age is important and I would commend to you the book *Love and Sex after Sixty* by Robert N. Butler, M.D., and Myrna I. Lewis, M.S.W. (New York: Ballantine Books,

1976, reprinted 1993). This is an informative, practical, and very readable volume.

In reality, questions about sexual activity in later years are more about attitudes, personal circumstances related to health and living arrangements, and available partners. "Should older people have sex lives? Are they even able to make love? Do they really want to? Is it appropriate— that is, 'normal' or 'decent'—or is sexual interest a sign of 'senility' and . . . poor judgment, or an embarrassing inability to adjust to aging with the proper restraint and resignation? How much less troubling it would be to accept the folklore of cookie-baking grandmothers who bustle about the kitchen making goodies for their loved ones while rocking-chair grandfathers puff on their pipes and reminisce. Idealized folk figures like these are not supposed to have sex lives of their own. After all, they are our parents and grandparents, not ordinary adults with the same needs and desires that we have."[3]

Attitudes are pervasive and quite damaging. Within the deep recesses of our minds lurks the myth that old age is sexless. Our parents don't do that sort of thing, and as for grandparents—well! Somewhere between birthday cards telling us forty is our prime and it's downhill thereafter and colloquialisms that include "dirty old men," older adults are told and often buy into the myth that old age is sexless.

What is pronounced good in our youth is no less good in our later years. To say less would be to deny an aspect of our embodiment, our humanness. To say less would be to say that at a certain age we become less than human, less than God intended us to be. Loving, the reaching out to the other in relationship, our communicating and communing, is basic to our humanity. The need to express this loving sexually does not recede with age. The way in which we express our loving sexually is dependent upon many factors in the psychological and physiological. Undoubtedly the giving and receiving of sexual love is complex. But this is true for the younger adult as well as the older adult. What younger adults do not have to deal with are the myths and prejudices (ageism), that promulgate a fear of growing older in a youthful culture. Older adults, who no longer have the societal and familial pressures of earlier years, should be encouraged to delight in their sexual selves in every appropriate and comfortable way.

Not all expressions of our sexuality are concerned with genital sexual activity. The body has many subtleties that can often be overlooked. From birth, the presence of another human being (parent) confirms being and well-being and confers personhood. Awareness of presence occurs in many ways and is not limited to our senses, although our experience of in-the-body does mean sight, sound, taste, smell, and touch as primary vehicles. As we grow and develop into individuated autonomous selves, our awareness of self and others becomes incorporated into being. We know ourselves to "be" in relation to others.

The loss of sight or hearing, faculty impairments that can occur at any stage in life (but are more common in later life) are isolating and engender an alienation from others. Alienation hits at the heart of our humanness. Created for community, created to know and experience self through others, older adults are confronted with hurdles that can sometimes feel insurmountable. Often the butt of jokes, regularly misunderstood, older adults can retreat to an inner world which serves only to reinforce a sense of alienation and isolation.

Communicating and communing from within our bodily, sexual selves can be as basic as seeing and hearing. These are two ways in which we experience ourselves to be in company, in relationship. These are two ways in which we know and are known. Relationship confirms our humanness and confers upon us personhood. The diminishment of one or both of our capacities to see or hear can have a profound effect on how we know ourselves to be persons. Of course, seeing and hearing can arouse that aspect of our sexuality which seeks to express itself in particular sexual activity. But seeing and hearing, essential parts of our embodiment, are by no means limited to these. I am very conscious of the empathy and passion aroused by contact with a child who cannot see or hear. We often go out of our way to communicate and commune with such little ones. Yet there seems to be less empathy or passion for the older adult who is without these capacities even though his or her experience is the same. Sensitivity to this aspect of our being-in-the-body is essential.

Touch is equally fundamental to, and as important for, our communicating and communing. The consequences of touch deprivation in infancy have been well studied and documented. High risk neonatal units (premature baby units) stress the importance of touch as a factor in growth. Throughout life the need to touch and be touched continues to be the primary vehicle through which we experience our humanness and a significant way in which personhood is conferred. Touch, perhaps more so than our other senses, conveys presence—a presence that can transcend barriers of seeing and hearing. The need for touch, sometimes described as "skin hunger," does not diminish with age. Indeed, it could be said that as our appetite and urgent need for engaging in genital sexual activity diminishes in intensity, the need to be physically touched by another human being and the need to touch another human being increases. Touch is always sensuous—of the senses. Touch is always potentially erotic. Touch is so much a part of our God-given embodiment that we find it to be a significant feature of Jesus' ministry and one of the significant ways people related to him. We touch from our body selves, from our maleness and femaleness. We receive touch as males and females. Touch is undeniably and inevitably sexual in nature.

Different societies and cultures define the parameters of appropriate human touching differently, including which parts of the human body may be appropriately or inappropriately touched. Within families there are unspoken rules about touching. Touch, because it is sensual and potentially erotic, has become something akin to a mine field in our time. Touch as a sign of simple affection can be misunderstood. This is true across the sexes and generations. Touch always requires permission and permission must never be assumed, whatever the age, whatever the gender. Sensitivity to context, a deep respect for the other, a genuine desire to preserve and affirm the human dignity of the other, are perhaps the broad guidelines for all human touching.

Older adults, along with the rest of humanity, are "skin hungry" beings. And older adults, unlike most of their younger counterparts are particularly prone to touch deprivation. The reasons are many and varied. The loss of a partner through death or divorce is probably the major source of touch deprivation in older adult life. Geographic mobility (and social mobility), separates kith and kin, perhaps our second most common source of touch, as never before. I was recently sitting in an airport and couldn't help but notice a heart-rending drama being quietly played out. Grandma was experiencing the leaving of daughter and an infant grandchild. When the flight was called there were deep breaths, tender hugs, and tears. As daughter and infant left it was grandmother's hand I noticed. It reached out into the empty space where they had been just a moment before.

Without suggesting that aging inevitably brings ill health, it is true that older adults are more inclined to experience chronic rather than acute illness. Providing tender care for a partner over a period of time can be a way to demonstrate love, esteem, and loyalty. Sometimes the need to be touched in return is not always possible.

Hospitalization, which has a certain publicness about it, can also inhibit the need to touch and be touched. The same may be true in retirement communities.

Finally, our changing physical appearance as we age can mean we feel untouchable and therefore are likely to recoil from touch. Our changing physical appearance can make us seem untouchable to others. Yet the reality remains that older adults, along with the rest of humanity, are skin-hungry beings. In our early years or our later years, touch is an integral part of all that it means to be "in the flesh."

Touch deprivation in older adults is not an accompaniment of the aging process. Touch deprivation in older adults should never be regarded as something which comes with increasing years and, like stiff knees and aching joints, needs to be accommodated and endured. Touch deprivation is what we consciously or unconsciously *do* to one another. Conversely, touch is therefore also something we may *give* to one another.

We do not need to be reminded of the demographic shift that is occurring. The fastest-growing segment of the population is over eighty-five years of age and this is expected to continue. Most often the response is to devise programs that focus on health care and social service needs. Ignoring sexuality issues does not mean they will disappear. As early as 1974, the National Council of Churches, the Synagogue Council of America, and the United States Catholic Conference issued an interfaith statement which concluded, "Sex education is not, however, only for the young, but is a life-long task whose aim is to help individuals develop their sexuality in a manner suited to their life stage."[4] As the baby boomers, who experienced a higher degree of sexual liberation than former generations, join the ranks of our graying population I suspect the church will be increasingly compelled to take more seriously this aspect of Christian education.

Questions for Thought and Discussion

1. Have you noticed changes in your own need to express yourself sexually?

2. Have the natural processes of aging impacted your communicating and communing? If so, how?

3. Singles (widowed, divorced, or never married) are likely to find fewer avenues for appropriate touching than others. If this has been your experience, can you articulate your difficulties and how you have, or have not, been able to meet this need?

4. How has the geographical distance of adult children and grandchildren influenced your life and sense of family connectedness?

5. An increasing number of older adults "parent" their grandchildren while parents work. If this has been your experience, can you share the pros and cons?

6. Is there a need for lifelong sex education? What would be the most appropriate context for this?

7. Do you agree that sexuality and the human need to express love in relationship does not diminish with age?

8. How much does the ability to hear and see influence

how you relate to other people, and, therefore, how does it affect the way you know yourself to be a human being?

9. If you wanted to show affection to someone in a hospital or nursing home setting, how would you go about it?

10. When is touch appropriate with another person, and when is it inappropriate?

11. In the midst of the sexual revolution, what should the church teach about sexuality? Should teaching differ for young people and older adults?

12. What would be the best, most acceptable way for a widow or widower with no family nearby to deal with her or his hungry skin?

3   Implications

For Couples

"Intimacy expresses the interpersonal capacity of a total life-sharing, not only through the Eros of passion, warmth and mature sexual encounter, but also through the agape of commitment, acceptance and self-disclosure. Intimacy cannot be reduced to tactility or even sexuality. It is a way of being and relating in closeness to the other in the life-process of creating a community."[5]

German Martinez's description of the depth of the marriage relationship is profound. Over a period of years patterns of relating develop between couples that are influenced by many internal and external factors. As the pressures of career ease and children leave home to establish their own homes, older couples face new challenges.

When the marriage vow, "till death us do part," was originally formulated, life expectancy was such that a marriage relationship would last twenty or at best thirty years. Golden wedding anniversaries are now common and the task of being open to the marriage partner in the "ebb and flow, the ups and downs, the fervor and dryness of life itself,"[6] requires commitment and work throughout life. While the person we married changes and grows, other factors such as change in lifestyle, reduced income, and amount of time spent with the spouse need to be considered. The comings and goings that shaped earlier days no longer set life's rhythms and routines. New rhythms and routines will begin to emerge. Adjustment and accommodation, essential features of the self-sacrificing agape love for the other, are both important. Married couples who reach retirement can look forward to perhaps thirty more years of married life together. In our youth, we planned our life—career, family, and home. In later life, planning is also necessary.

Patterns of sexual intimacy established over a lifetime may or may not change in later life. Being able to speak openly about intimacy is vital. This may seem obvious, but in long-term relationships much can be assumed. Habits of silence because we think we know what the other is thinking may turn into dissatisfactions and barriers. Depth of communion is most often a result of meaningful dialogue. The communication of desires and frustrations will help us avoid unmet expectations, which can be as much part of later life as in our earlier years. Cherished rituals can become alive and charged with meaning. The simple intimacy of sharing a meal together has deeply spiritual implications. This act of communicating and communing lies at the heart of our worship and our home. Mealtimes, as occasions for sharing and caring, and making space for the other, can take on a sacramental quality. Discovering ever new opportunities to express care and concern for a partner can become a delightful adventure when romanticism is reclaimed in maturity.

Questions for Thought and Discussion
1. How can the church assist couples with their continued growth as older married couples? How can the church in its rituals recognize and enhance the depth of the marriage relationship?
2. Observe your church's worship service and ask yourself, "Which age group and/or family configuration is the focus of the worship and programming in our church?"
3. Do you think it would be appropriate for the church to devise marriage vows for older persons?
4. If you were on a committee to devise reaffirmation of marriage vows for persons celebrating their fiftieth wedding anniversary, what would be included?

For Singles

Barbara P. Payne has commented, "Congregations have not only been youth and male orientated, but couple and family orientated. Congregations have been characterized by a 'Noah's ark' syndrome in which all are expected to enter two by two. This Noah's ark syndrome is a sex-negativism that places primacy on sexual activity as procreation. Important as this aspect of sexuality is, it is age-specific for women and does not represent the total experience of human sexuality"[7]

The statistics she goes on to quote are illuminating. In 1984, 40 percent of adults age sixty-five and older were married. Twice as many older men were likely to be married than older women. There were five times as many widows as widowers and the disparity increases at older ages. In 1985, 68 percent of women over seventy-five were widowed compared to less than 23 percent of men over age seventy-five (a disparity partly related to age-specific death rates in older men and the tendency to marry younger women). Divorce among older people has increased faster than the older population as a whole in the past twenty years. Among the future elderly (men and women), approximately one-half will have been divorced by the time they reach the age of seventy-five.

A small number (less than 8 percent) of older persons never marry. However, since many young adults are delaying or rejecting marriage, the number of never-married older persons can be expected to increase. There is a disparity between the longevity of women and men. Women tend to live longer than men by approximately eight to ten years. By age sixty-five, women outnumber men three to two. In 1984, among those over the age of eighty-five, there were forty men for every one hundred women.[8]

Given that older adults do not become nonsexual beings when they reach a particular age, the implications of these statistics are disturbing. Establishing communicating and communing relationships in later life would appear to be increasingly difficult with age, more so for women than men. Women tend to relate to friends and find meaning and fulfillment in same-sex activities and organizations. In later life women may value the independence that newly acquired singleness affords. This may also be true of older men, although the statistics would indicate they prefer to seek marriage relationships.

Those older adults who do establish relationships and seek marriage can become the butt of jokes, the assumption being that their relationship is more about platonic companionship than sexual interest. Gerontologists dispute this, saying that sexual interest is as much part of older adult life as earlier life. Finding appropriate ways to express this is an essential ingredient to wholeness and well-being. While the shared life, home, and financial resources of older persons may mean marriage is an attractive prospect, this may not always be the case. I am acquainted with a couple in their early seventies who have dated for several years. Both were widowed in their late fifties. The woman's husband had made adequate financial provision for their future through his career pension. The pension would be forfeited should she remarry. Pragmatic choices may mean forced singleness rather than chosen singleness. Lack of available partners may force singleness. The financial dilemmas older adults face can mean marriage is not an option—but is cohabitation an alternative?

Questions for Thought and Discussion
  1. How do single older adults recognize their own "skin-hungry-ness?"
  2. In your opinion, do single persons (divorced, widowed, single by choice, etc.) find the church a welcoming community?
  3. Would you agree that it is acceptable for two older per-

sons (male and female) to live together, though unmarried, if they are in a financial dilemma brought on by pension rules and guidelines that would cut off income were they to get married, making it impossible for them to make it financially?

For Those Living in Retirement Communities
In past years there was an unspoken assumption that aging parents would be cared for by children. This is no longer the case. A mobile society, a more fragile notion of the extended family, and demographic facts, combined with the fact that we live longer and are healthier, mean both change in circumstance and expectation. Retirement communities are increasingly part of older adult life and many have much to offer. Independent living in community can be relationally rewarding. The opportunities for romance and appropriate sexual expression can be a nurturing feature of such communities. When independent living is no longer an option for couples the picture can change.

Some retirement communities make provision for married couples and the intimacy shared throughout life is continued. Sadly, this is not always so and married couples may find they have separate beds or even separate rooms. Opportunities for moments of intimacy may be replaced by management and efficiency concerns. Behind this lies the myth that old age is sexless. When singles (unmarried, widowed, and divorced) enter retirement communities and need more care than they previously did, developing relationships can be regarded with suspicion and derision. The publicness of such living does not afford many moments of privacy. The need for intimate care (bathing and toilet needs), from caregivers can be a further assault on our personhood, of which our sexuality is an integral part. Sexual arousal, which intimate care can stimulate, is healthy and normal. Preserving dignity and awareness that our sexuality does not change with age need to be concerns that are addressed by those providing care in such facilities.

Questions for Thought and Discussion
1. How can retirement communities and nursing facilities provide situations whereby the intimacy and "touch" needs of all residents can be addressed? Would such actions be acceptable to society at large?
2. What can the church do to educate its members concerning the continuing need for older persons to experience touch and intimacy?

For Adult Children
I recall seeing a TV special a few years ago in which Katharine Hepburn played an older adult who fell in love with and married her physician. That her doctor was Jewish did complicate matters, but the real angst the couple faced was due to their grown children. "It's ridiculous at your age, unseemly even!" portrays the difficulty many of us have with the notion that our parents or grandparents

are ordinary sexual beings like us. In our heads we know they must be or we would not be alive. Our feelings may tell another story. Perhaps because sexuality is so intensely personal and for many, surrounded by learned taboos, accepting that our parents are quite capable of falling in love and wanting to express this sexually can be an immense hurdle. When property and finance enter the equation much hurt can arise. Rightly or wrongly, grown children may have the prospect of a legacy in their mind, and a new spouse would be perceived as a threat. As a pastor, I have witnessed the pain that can be engendered for all concerned. As we live longer, healthier lives this scenario will possibly become more familiar. I wonder if we are prepared for the ramifications of the age-wave which is undoubtedly upon us.

Questions for Thought and Discussion
1. Do you know of a situation where adult children have found it difficult to cope with their parent developing new relationships with the opposite sex? What factors were involved?
2. What can the church do to ease the tensions between adult children and their parents in circumstances where the parent plans to remarry and the adult children cannot understand it and are opposed to the marriage?

For Churches
A cursory glance around many local church congregations will tell us that our fellowship is, like society in general, aging.

While many denominations are aware of this and are devising older adult programs, there is still little discussion on the need for sexual intimacy in later life. Sex and the older adult, as Barbara P. Payne's article suggested, is still a laughing matter in religion. If the church is to take seriously sexual identity as an integral part of our human createdness, this must be addressed. Honest and reliable information, and open discussion in affirming and secure contexts, can be provided by the church, the living embodiment of Christ.

The church also needs to take into account the statistics. The shift from youth to adult congregations has already occurred. The next shift is likely to be to older adult congregations. Are we using our older lay and ordained members to their fullest? The statistics also indicate women are likely to live longer than men, yet our prevailing church cultures are quite often male and youth orientated. Can we rise to the challenge this will present to programming?

Pastoral care and social support among our older adult congregations will need to include singles groups that are affirming and morale-enhancing, marital counseling that is geared toward sexuality in older adult life, and marriage or remarriage in later life. Couples who have spent a lifetime in a marriage relationship may also have particular needs—marriage enrichment can be useful at any stage or age.

The skin hunger and alienation brought on by hearing and sight loss can be met by a sensitivity on the part of the whole congregation, not simply those who offer care. Regular friendship visiting to those in retirement communities needs to be a well-organized ministry of the congregation.

There are different levels of care support needed in retirement communities. Independent living may well be enhanced by friendship visiting, although my experience with the early older adult years leads me to wonder how they managed during their younger years to fit in the time to pursue a career, or be part-time or fulltime homemaker! Retired living that needs supportive and structured care can bring in its wake a much smaller worldview. As one octogenarian remarked to me, "When you get older, your family grows, but your friends get fewer." In our mobile society, that often separates grown children from parents and that most often has witnessed the disintegration of the extended family, the friendship visiting of the living body of Christ, of which we the church are a part, may be a significant and important factor in preventing the very real isolation of "a family that grows" and "friends who become fewer."

Perhaps more than all of these, the church needs to consider the implications of aging and sexuality in its articulation of faith and ritual. Liturgies that celebrate older life, including sexuality, are urgently required.

Questions for Thought and Discussion
1. How can the church be made aware of the alienation caused by skin hunger and hearing and sight losses?
2. How can the church address the fact that churches for the most part view sex for older persons as a laughing matter, not to be discussed within the walls of the church?

3. In view of the fact that more than one-third of all church members are over age sixty-five, and that most are women, how do you explain the fact that the focus of the programming of the church is on youth?

4   Where Do We Go from Here?

I have attempted to invite personal thought and, hopefully, group sharing and discussion about a deeply personal subject—that is, what it means to be a created human being. This necessarily means our physical sexual being, our whole body-selves. I have identified what I consider to be some signposts, ways toward integration, and how I personally believe God is currently challenging us. I am aware that people who read this book may not be from the '60s generation, but, from my own pastoral experience, the issues raised are common to all older adults. It would be a pity if, having spent time discussing this very personal subject, constructive ways forward were not identified. So where do we go from here?

Questions for Thought and Discussion
1. Was it helpful to think about sexuality and your own stage in the aging process?
2. Was it helpful to talk about your own aging and sexuality in a group?
3. What difference do you think the nature of your thinking makes in terms of relating?
4. What ideas for church care and programs would

your group suggest? Make a list of these ideas and offer them to the session of your congregation.

5. If, in your group discussions, you have developed a model for such care and programming that could work in your congregation, write it down and share it with other congregations in your presbytery.

6. Has your group identified stages and transitions in older adult life that need to be recognized and celebrated in the liturgy and worship of the congregation? Work with your congregation's worship committee in planning a celebration service that is inclusive of older married couples, older single persons, grandparents raising children, and grandchildren as well as youth and young adults.

7. If you want to take this a step further, establish support groups for the various transitions of life experiences shared by all persons. When you have developed a working model for support groups, write it down and share it with other congregations in your presbytery.

Notes

1. James Nelson, *Embodiment* (Minneapolis: Augsburg Publishing House, 1978), 18.
2. Paul Ricoeur, "Wonder, Eroticism and Enigma" in *Sexuality and Identity*, ed. H. Ruitenbeek (New York: Dell, 1970), 13.
3. R. N. Butler and M. I. Lewis, *Love and Sex after Sixty* (New York: Ballantine Books, 1976; reprinted 1993), 5–6.
4. Quoted by Barbara P. Payne, "Sex and the Elderly: No Laughing Matter in Religion," in *Christian Perspectives on Sexuality and Gender*, ed. Elizabeth Stuart and Adrian Thatcher (Grand Rapids; Wm. B. Eerdmans Publishing Co., 1996), 369.
5. German Martinez, "Marriage as Worship: A Theological Analogy," in Thatcher and Stuart, eds., *Christian Perspectives on Sexuality and Gender*, 188.
6. Ibid., 189.
7. Payne, "Sex and the Elderly," 371.
8. Ibid., 370–71.

Resources

1. The National Association of Social Workers, 750 First Street, NE, Washington, DC 20002.
2. The American Psychological Association, 1200 17th Street, NW, Washington, DC 20036.
3. The National Mental Health Association, 1021 Prince Street, Alexandria, VA 22314.
4. Family Service America, 11700 West Lake Park Drive, Milwaukee, WI 53224.
5. The National Caucus on the Black Aged, 2801 14th Street, NW, First Floor, Washington, DC 20009.
6. The American Association for Marriage and Family Therapy, 1100 7th Street, NW, 10th Floor, Washington, DC 20036.
7. The American Association of Sex Educators, Counselors, and Therapists, 435 North Michigan Avenue, Suite 1717, Chicago, IL 60611.
8. Masters and Johnson Institute, 24 South Kingshighway Boulevard, St. Louis, MO 63108.
9. The Sex Information and Education Council of the United States, 32 Washington Place, Room 52, New York University, New York, NY 10003.
10. The American Geriatrics Society, 770 Lexington Avenue, Suite 400, New York, NY 10021.

Appendix

In the October/November 1998 issue of *NCOA Networks*, a publication of the National Council on the Aging (409 Third Street SW, Washington, DC 20024), an article appeared concerning a major study of older adults and sexuality. With permission from NCOA, the entire article is reprinted here for your information.

NCOA Unveils Major Study of Seniors and Sexuality
by Neal E. Cutler, Ph.D.

Older men and women know it and professionals in the field of aging know it, but many younger people and even middle-agers don't fully understand that sexual interest and sexual activity continue well into older age.

In 1994, a research team from the University of Chicago published the results of a national study titled *Sex in America*, a carefully planned and skillfully executed social scientific research project. The book's subtitle, *A Definitive Survey*, is fairly accurate—except that the research sampled only adults through age 59!

To shed light on this important area of aging in contemporary American life, The National Council on the Aging (NCOA) recently completed a major national survey of men and women age 60 and older. The NCOA study, *Healthy Sexuality and Vital Aging*, is based on a representative survey of 1300 people in the United States and was conducted by Roper Starch Worldwide. The study was supported by an unrestricted grant from Pfizer Inc.

Our study begins by looking at the qualities that older men and women look for in their romantic partners. On several such qualities, there emerged what can be called a national consensus—qualities that a vast majority (90% or more) of both men and women agreed were important in choosing a partner: a high moral character, a pleasant personality, a good sense of humor, and intelligence.

The study did find, however, some interesting differences between men and women. In particular, more women than men seek financial security in a partner (85% of women, 56% of men) and seek a partner who observes a religious faith (72% of women, 58% of men). On the other hand, more men than women seek a partner who likes to have sex (76% of men, 46% of women) and a partner who has an attractive body shape (67% of men, 48% of women).

Healthy Sexuality and Vital Aging found that about half (48%) of Americans age 60 and over are sexually active, that is, engage in some form of sex at least once a month. Overall, more men than women said they are sexually active (61% of men and 37% of women). A majority of Americans who are in their 60s are sexually active (71% of men and 51% of women). Fewer respondents in their 70s and 80s said they are sexually active; considerably more men than women in these age groups said they are sexually active.

Thirty-nine percent of respondents said they are satisfied with the amount of sex they currently have, and another 39%

said they want more frequent sex. Men were more than twice as likely as women to report wanting more sex (56 percent vs. 25 percent). Only 4% of the seniors said they want less. Among older people with current sex partners, 71% said that maintaining an active sex life is important to their relationships.

Sixty-one percent of all older men and women say that their sex life today is either physically more satisfying or unchanged compared to when they were in their 40s. Thirty-seven percent said their sex life is less satisfying physically. When asked about the emotional satisfaction of their sex life, half of all older respondents said they are more satisfied or unchanged compared to when they were in their 40s. Thirty-seven percent said that their sex life is less satisfying emotionally.

Quizzed about several topics related to sex and health, respondents correctly answered many questions but were unsure about others. Four out of five (81%) correctly agreed with the statement that older people are just as susceptible to sexually transmitted diseases—such as AIDS —as younger people.

Most respondents (53%) disagreed with the statement that women have less sexual desire after menopause (14% agreed and 27% were unsure). Women were more likely to disagree than men (44% of men, 60% of women) and more men were unsure (35% of men, 20% of women). There was more uncertainty, however, about the statement "The loss of the ability to get an erection is an inevitable part of growing older" (27% (correctly) agreed, 36% disagreed, 30% were unsure).

Overall, the NCOA's 1998 *Healthy Sexuality and Vital Aging* national survey finds that both sexual interest and sexual activity are alive and well in contemporary older America. Most older men and women prefer more rather than less sexual activity, and large proportions find as much or more satisfaction with their sex life today as compared to when they were forty. At the same time, the study has identified a number of areas of uncertainty and misinformation regarding aging and sexuality.

Neal E. Cutler, Ph.D., is director of survey research at NCOA and holds the Joseph Boettner/Davis Gregg Chair of Financial Gerontology at Widener University.

(Copyright by The National Council on the Aging, 1998. Reprinted by permission.)